River of Stars

Poems

William K. Leutz

Three Black Spruce Publishing

2021

River of Stars: Poems

Published by: Three Black Spruce Publishing

Text copyright © 2021 by William K. Leutz

All rights reserved. No part of this book may be used or reproduced in any manner whatsoever without written permission except in the case of brief quotations embodied in critical articles and reviews. For information, please address William K. Leutz at 3blkspruce@gmail.com

Cover image and poem illustrations by Shutterstock
Star image designed by rawpixel.com / Freepik

ISBN: 978-1-7375571-0-4
Library of Congress: 2021914066

Publisher's Cataloging-in-Publication data
Names: Leutz, William K., author.
Title: River of stars : poems / William K. Leutz.
Description: Clarklake, MI: Three Black Spruce Publishing, 2021.
Identifiers: LCCN: 2021914066 | ISBN: 978-1-7375571-0-4 (hardcover) | 978-1-7375571-1-1 (paperback) | 978-1-7375571-2-8 (ebook)
Subjects: LCSH Poetry, American. | BISAC POETRY / General
Classification: LCC PS3612.E9223 R58 2021 | DDC 811.6--dc23

Dedicated To

Barbara K. Leutz
19 December 1935 – 2 February 2012

*"Those who love
remain with us, for
love itself lives on.*

*Cherished memories never fade
because they're gone.*

*Those we love can never be
more than a thought apart,
for as long as there is memory
they'll live on in our hearts."*

Barbara Koerner Leutz - 2008

Table of Contents

Author's Introduction

I
Rhythms

Cycles	3
Lake Legacy	4
Sunday Morning	6
Autumn Drought	7
The River Flowing	8
Crossing the Plains	10
After the Family was Gone	16
Broken Dream	17
Empty Silo	18
Grass Fire	19
Dawn Visit	20
Time's Bell	21
Bare Branches	22
National Senility	23
Sandhill Crane	24
The Dancer's Skirt	25
First Snowfall	26
Summer Dawn	28
The Currents of History	29
Rhinoceros	30

II
Myths

Beyond the Fields We Know 35
Mythic Purity 36
Navajo Weaver 38
The River of Stars 39
The Song of the Selkie 40
Youth's Passage 43
Night's Mysteries 44
Hunter and Hound 46
Seasons at Edo 47
Hidden Woman 48
The Dancing Stars 49
Autumn Morning 50
Destiny 51
Voices 52

III
Memories

Walking with Grandad 55
Questions of a Ten-acre Woods 56
Fjord Wings 57
The Old Mill 58
A Blue Wax Day 59
Quiet Evening 60
All my Life there has been Music 62
Oman 64
Carcassonne 65
Campfire Reflections 66
Old Flames 68
Goldfinch 69
Anniversary 70
We Survived It 71
Golden Pagoda 72
Remembering Your Birthday 74

IV
Morning Thoughts

Three AM / Quiet Forest 77
Southbound Geese / Wind in the Pines 78
Bright Days / Daily Life 79
Two Thoughts on Non-Attachment 80
Cherry Season / Great Wave of Kanagawa 81
The Cusp of Now / December Stories 82
Norwegian Cliffs 83
Dance of Time 84
Perception's Flower 85
The Horns of Selene 86
This Moment of You 87
Mindful 88
Truth and Beauty 89
Season's Ending 90

About the Author 93

Introduction

Although I still have copies of a few poems written for grammar school and high school English assignments that were saved from oblivion by my well-meaning mother, I didn't begin seriously writing until 1982. At that time, living and working in Norway, I found more time to appreciate the beauty of that country, as well as the words I was reading in English and Norwegian literature. Over the years, a few poems have found their way into the public forum through small journals, small-town newspapers, or electronic media.

My first book, entitled *The Clams are Still Baking: Memories of Clark Lake*, presented a collection of family stories and memories, as well as a few poems, associated with 114 years, and three generations of summers on Clark's Lake. It was published by Authorhouse in 2013.

What Do You See: Poems of Perception was published by Hawkeye Publishers in 2019. This collection of poetry draws inspiration from many sources in the realm of spiritual literature including, but not limited to, a small selection of Biblical references, assorted Zen writers, the Dao De Ching, and the Sufi poetry of Jaladdin Rumi and Haifez of Shiraz. For general reference, these two books can be found at <amazon.com/author/williamkleutz>.

In this present collection, I have brought together a broader range of poetry, covering the last 38 years. The first part of this book, sections I, II, and III, are collections of the subjects that seem to inform my writing most; the cycles of life, ancient myths, and personal memories.

In 2017, after finding repeated references to the work of the Chinese 9th Century Daoist poet Du Fu, I decided to find and read some of his work. This led to the discovery and reading of poets of the same era; Lin Biao, and Han Shan (known as Cold Mountain). Continuing in this tradition, I purchased *The Mountain Poems of Stonehouse (Shih Wu)*, translation and commentary by Bill Porter, under his Chinese name of Chi Song (Red Pine) in 2019. Porter was also translator of an earlier book of Han Shan's poetry which I already had in my library. Unlike the first three poets, Shih Wu was a 14th century Buddhist hermit. I began reading these works before I went to sleep at night. Often waking around 3am, poetry, mostly in the Chinese eight line, seven-syllable form, or Japanese Tanka, materialized. These poems, a continuation of the work in *What Do You See*, are included in Section IV.

Acknowledgements of assistance needs to be made for the support of my family - sister's Elizabeth (Betsy) Leutz Frazen and Ann Leutz Swain, and my late wife, Joyce Armstrong-Leutz. I wish that my father and my oldest sister Barbara, both fellow writers of verse who have now passed, were able to enjoy this publication. I also owe a great deal to editorial assistance, provided on the various past incarnations of this collection, from Brandi George, Michelle Battiste, and Wilma Ward Nichols. And finally, I wish to express my appreciation to Joan Moore Shropshire for her help with the final editing and to Connie Huddleston for her invaluable assistance in finalizing this volume. Without these colleagues and friends, this book would never have been finished.

William K. Leutz

I
Rhythms

Cycles

The lake lies frozen
beneath the Cold Moon.
Its surface, like polished glass,
reflects the thousand stars.

Houses that stood full
beneath the blue sky of July
are empty now;
spoiled pensioners seeking the sun.

Children who played in its water
in the sunny days of youth,
make pilgrimage to its source
in the solstice of their life.

The wheel of ages
circles endlessly in the skies,
on the earth,
and in the ways of man.

Lake Legacy

For one reason or another,
Dad never lived here year-around,
although he often dreamed of retiring here,
with that view of the setting sun
and the soft breezes on his face,

I see his laughing face
one hundred years ago,
playing with his cousins
on an overturned fishing boat
in the shallows of the lake.

Each year they came
from the city's growing crowds
to share the beauty and the joy
of this spring-fed paradise.

First their parents rented
a week or two each year,
in one of the many cottages
that spun out from the hub
that was the Eagle Point Hotel.

Then, some ninety years ago
his aunt and uncle bought one
that stood just down the shore
from the rocking chairs
on the old Hotel's wooden porch.

Years later,
when all four of those young boys
had grown to men,
they still brought their families back
to where their summer roots ran deep.

He used to say that he had
sipped the water from the clear springs
every year of his life except the first.
A generation later, I say the same.

Now, in my seventh decade,
after wandering the wide world,
the legacy has come full circle
for, at last, I am living his dream.

Sunday Morning

It's early Sunday morning in the hollow house,
and I lie on the downstairs couch
with poetry beside me, while outside,
from her wicker home beneath the porch,
the Phoebe sings two note prayers
to the rising sun for her three children,
still sleeping in their round china wombs.

In a crabapple tree, across the misted pond,
the cardinal returns his benediction.
No other sound but the rumbling of my tired brain,
stumbling across these scattered words;
until the music of silence ends
as the kitchen clock chimes eight times,
and the planned day begins.

Autumn Drought

The grey October dawn
spreads slowly
across the plains,
casting softened shadows
of a gnarled and wind-torn oak,
on the striped, brown, blanket
of sun-blasted grass.
The summer drought
has sent its gaping fissures
crazing the red earth
between the dead blades.
The stock pond stands too low;
as if the moon
had sent some massive tide
to draw the waters out
to bathe her dry and sunburnt face.
Frogs dig down into the mud
to shade their tender skins,
while turtles venture out
upon dry land to find a safer home,
and in the deepest holes
the families of fish
have congregated, churning
the mire for chum.
All life waits, panting.
for that first, moist, breath
of autumn rain.

The River Flowing
Ode to the Arkansas

Low winter flow,
placid water reflects the sky,
empty cottonwoods arch above the shore
while here and there a scattered oak
still bears the battered cloak of last year's leaves.

Within the stream, small island bars
drape a crackled scarf of cat-ice
around their barren shoulders,
while their sand-brown skin is dusted
with the snow of gulls.

Just months ago, this river roared
with all the strength of spring,
filled to the gills, the floodgates
of the dams were opened wide
to feed its racing hunger.

Bank to bank it paced,
and where the banks were low
it spread across the land
like a wrinkled gray garment.
Still the storms spread rain
across the plains of Kansas.

From spring to fall to spring,
from flood to drought to flood,
the river is this land.
No memory of man exists
in which it does not tie
the mountains to the sea.

Through days that leave a trickle
weaving through expanse of dampened sand,
to floods that sweep across the sodden land,
its waters still bring life and death
as mankind reaches out
to cross the river of the stars.

Crossing the Plains

I - New Mexico, February 1992

Throughout the night's dark solitude
the black macadam roles beneath
my wheels, bounded by white ribbons
that define the tar-dark distance.

The right runs smoothly on into
the vortex of the endless way
while, on the left, its broken cousin
flies – a flashing beacon dancing

down the center of the road.
Ahead the perfect moon has left
its harbor in the valleys of
the distant mountains.

And as it sails its midnight sea,
its pearl-gray light, as inverse shadow,
creeps across the sliding landscape,
ghostlike in the corner of my eye.

II - Alberta, February 1994

The Northern Plains roll like ocean
swells towards a distant shoreline.
Above that coast, white mountains
rise to block the edge of sight.

Bare, rock-layered hillsides line
the road like long, brown
wave-crests, breaking
as we approach the foot-hilled shore.

Tall groves of pine reach up,
green kelp beds
sheltering the life
of a rocky wind-blown coast.

A great bay opens wide
into the open valley of
the Bow River's gravel bed,
surrounded by its massive peaks.

High angled strata, climbing across
the cliffs above the river's bend,
create a crenelated fortress
to protect this mountain harbor.

While in the valley, the highway
wanders north between a stockade built
of pines, slender and straight,
holding back the wildness of the forest.

III – Oklahoma, March 1999

Late winter in the Central Plains.
Brown grasses stretch into
the blue-gray haze of lands edge.
An undulating land broken

by a few old oaks,
barren branches reaching
into the clear blue sky.
A red-tailed hawk perches in the crown,

sharp eyes searching for prey
running through the dried grasses.
Branches already touched
with the soft saffron hues of early buds,

soon will sharpen into
the bright new green of spring's
first leaves before the dust-filled
winds of summer's heat

soften that sheen
into the dull green-browns of June.
Strewn across the level plains,
green squares of winter wheat,

seem bright enough to stun the eye.
Brown cattle scatter across the open plains
like summer freckles,
seeking the freshest grass.

Skeletal horseheads bob,
oil field pumps,
sipping the black blood of the land
like metal mosquitoes.

IV – Kansas, March 2001

The weathered gray barn,
red-roofed,
stands forlorn
in the emptiness.

A solitary horse grazes
slowly, along a windswept fence.
Wooden windmills stand
stark against the unforgiving sky.

Curves of contour plowing
Flow in arabesques around brown hills.
High in the sky, fresh contrails
etch white rails across the continent

while, beneath, gray asphalt
reaches for the horizon,
its tar-filled cracks scrolling
the liquid black ink of Arabic poetry.

The setting sun
throws eastern reaching shadows
from the red-dirt walls
of every wandering stream-bed,

White columns of grain elevators cluster
where towns followed the railroad across the vacant prairie,
rising like bleached volcanic dikes
above a steel-shod fault-line.

Each town seems protected
by its bulbous water tower
standing on stilted legs,
a Martian machine from the mind of H.G. Wells.

And here and there the shattered wrecks
of tractors and combines poke from the hillsides;
bones of rust and green dinosaurs
trapped in the tar pits of obsolescence.

V

Four visions of the plains,
seen from behind the windshield
of a speeding car
racing from nowhere to nowhere.

Imagine instead this world
before the white ships came.
No fields or furrows
lying beneath the sun;

no heaps of rusted metal,
no roads except the riverbeds
laddering across the plains
from west to east;
just brown grass hills
beneath a timeless dome
in which a saffron sun
bakes the arid land.

Hawk soared aloft,
Prairie Grouse boomed below,
Coyote howled at night,
and the thunder of stampeding buffalo
echoed through the eons.

Is it better now than then?
Ask me not.
Ask instead the antelope
that roamed free.
Ask the prairie dog
that honeycombed its land.

Ask the Great Mystery
that placed it here
to serve all the creatures of
His endless imagination.

After the Family was Gone

Months later, after the family was gone,
after the trip of homage to Blue River,
after the pilgrimage to other rivers,
in other states, in other lands,
you came back to me.

In my dream-vision, standing on a lanai
above a beach at Monterey that we never visited,
I saw you walk by, beachcombing,
in that old, blue knit, one piece, bathing suit
you wore to work in the garden.

Turning your head,
flashing that joyous smile,
and with a brief wave of the hand,
you continued walking
down that beach outside of time.

Broken Dream

Brokenly, the dream
wandered through
in jumbled pieces, a jigsaw puzzle
poured from the box to the tabletop,
collage of colored emotions,
waiting to be glued up.

- High school stadium
  at a football game with Dad
- Following a braided stream
  through a grassy field,
  before the school was built,
- Wandering across
  a frozen lake at night
- Phone call of a death

And I, still sleepless,
beneath the tick
of the overhead fan.

Empty Silo

The empty silo rises
roofless above the old
barn's wind-blown floor,
pasture stone and rotting mortar,
grey against the sky of summer.

Ivy, reaching for the sun,
drapes its ash-grey shoulder,
while windows, like empty eyes,
peep between the vines.

Once filled with corn stalks
to feed the cattle
through the cold winter,
it now stands empty,

Only a lone oak sapling,
refuse of a grey squirrel's lost lunch,
searches upward for life
from deep within the prison of its stone tower.

Grass Fire

Hot, dry, autumn days,
when prairie winds whip across
the knotted fields of sun-dried grasses;
a lightening stroke,
a casual spark,
a discarded cigarette,
sunlight through a broken bottle,
who knows what simple act
sets the red buffalo stampeding
down the long wind-trail;
clouds of gray-white smoke
mark his passing from afar,
while near at hand,
the blackened earth
bears the mark of his fiery hooves.

Dawn Visit

A statue in stillness
poised on the wooden dock,
or slowly striding through the shallows,
he arrives in the morning
to vie with the yearling bass
for the sweetness of sand shiners
that school between the docks;
three-toed dinosaur tracks
press into the rippled sand
swept back into the lake
by wind-driven waves.

Like a thin-legged pedagogue
clad in slate-grey cutaways
and a rumpled dress shirt,
he startles as I descend the steps.
Ungainly at first, the heron lifts
on that five-foot wingspan
to glide soundlessly
into the mists.

Time's Bell

Yes, you are right.
It is that time of night
to out the light
and close the book
of words that shook
my heart
apart.

As darkness comes
with all the pomp
of silent drums,
the wind song seeps
around the corners
of reluctant sleep
until oblivion hums
hypnotic spells
dredged up from deepest wells.

Your sadness rises
from the depths,
in all its shapes
and all its sizes,
where dreams of empty floors
and shattered doors
echo the bell chimes
of unending time.

Bare Branches

High, in bare branches
of the old basswood,
the eagle rests,
his clear eyes scanning the lake.

White head, white tail,
black suit between.

Does he still see the old days
when the water was clear,
only the occasional birch canoe,
garpike rolling,
bass rising to the fly?

National Senility

Two hundred thirty years since birth,
one hundred since the first steps of hegemony,
age takes its toll.

First lessons are lost in the mists of time.
Principles are pared away by expedience.
Integrity suffers the slow death of starvation.

Madness runs through the corridors of power,
bullies bluster, week men weep, the greedy grasp,
democracy diminishes into chaos.

Blessingless, the poor have lost their kingdom,
the meek have no inheritance,
the mourners find no comfort,
mercy and purity are words without meaning.

And all the while the silent masses watch,
too complacent to retake the reins
while the foundered horse stumbles in the dark.

Sandhill Crane

Stork-like, striding on long stems
in brown jacket and red cap,
peering through round reed
and sharp-edged sedge,
the crane stalks the young frog
along the marshes fringe;
They have returned to the prairies,
thriving in fresh mowed fields,
wheeling above in fall skies.

The Dancer's Skirt

The dervish spins in ecstasy.
But Oh! To be his whirling skirt;
round by dizzying round,
lifted by the force of spinning,
flowing lightly in the air
in praise of timeless Love.

First Snowfall
Jenks, Oklahoma – December 2000

I woke last night to hear the hand of winter
scatter sleet across the window pane,
while wind's whine came whistling through the eaves;
and in the morning found the year's first snow
strewn wetly on the pasture and the barn.
The roan, the pinto and the gray were pawing at this covering,
in hopes of finding, here and there,
a slender blade of breakfast to offset the cold.

As I left the house, their ears all raised
to hear my footsteps on the wooden porch,
and then, heads up, they all came trotting in,
fetlocks fringed with snow and nostrils steaming
from warm breath against the frigid air.
They came in hopes of grain, a flake of hay,
and then, perhaps a pat upon the withers,
to warm them from their long night.

Although the dogs all romp upon the snow,
the horses seem to find it less appealing.
Of course, the dogs all slept upon warm beds
within the shelter of the heated house,
while all night long the horses knew the storm
first hand. The barn might give some shelter from
the falling snow, or from the wind, but nothing
shielded them from the bitter cold.
A cold that marks the ending of the year;
As every year must start in cold and end
in cold, and only find its heat in middle age.

In this millennial year, the world
still watches as the seasons turn around the sun.
We watch to see new life in spring, as trees
fill up with leaves, and foals and calves
are dropped in pastures all around.
As they grow, the summer's days speed by
while fruits and berries ripen on the vine.
Fall comes and harvest feeds the land, before
the winter drives life back into the ground.

Now we feed the stock, and feed ourselves,
on all the produce of that passing year;
just as they did a thousand years ago.
Stepping back a thousand years a go
until the dawning of our race, the season's
hold on us, and on our lives, remains unchanged
for all our vaunted age and its technology.

    We grow within the confines of creation
    and let its music carry us along,
    but though we seek to find some moderation,
    we cannot change the rhythm of its song.

Summer Dawn

Summer dawn.
The sky is a faded blue;
beneath, the reflecting lake,
a darker hue.

In between, the rising sun
has brushed the western shore
with magenta ink,
fading upward to a petal pink.

While from its tiny perch,
nestled deep within the heavy spruce,
the wren sings "Hosanna!"
for the end of night.

The Currents of History

The things that hold a memory
of those no longer here:

- The scent of lilacs in spring,
- The mournful call of a loon at night,
- The taste of cinnamon in hot coffee,
- The smell of horse....

But there is no such power
in the things themselves.

The heart holds the emotion,
and we are swept away in its tide.

Rhinoceros

Rhinoceros, pelican, dolphin,
would they miss us were we gone?
Probably not. In their freedom
from the invisible cage of time
we are insignificant except
as a hazard, predator, killer.

Would we miss them?
Probably not. In the arrogance
of our self-assured insecurity
we attach no importance
to that which is not our ego.

We, who do not understand
a different culture, a fellow human
who simply speaks a different language,
how can we assume to understand?
a different species, family, phylum?
How can we assume superiority?
over that with which we cannot communicate?

We do so by the simple expedience
of saying it is their weakness not ours,
by demanding that all communication
must be on our terms, in our time,
or it is non-existent.

We do so by the perceived
power of a judgment made
without witness or foundation.
Such imagined superiority exists
only by definition of the term,
acknowledged by an ego
that cannot bear the alternative.

II
Myths

Beyond the Fields We Know
(In Remembrance of Edmund, Lord Dunsany)

I wandered once beyond the fields we know
into Illusion's home, the Land of Dreams,
and many wonders found within its bounds.
Now often, when I come to sleep, it seems
that I recall the mighty Yann's broad flow

as falling from its distant mountain peaks,
it winds beneath the silver morning light.
From bank to bank re-echo forest sounds
of painted birds that sing from dawn to night,
while idle sailors ride its stream to seek

their fortune in great cities on its plains.
I see the ivory gate that once had graced
the walls of Perdondaris in its prime;
where still the faint perfume and haunting face
of Saranoora, dancing, forges chains

about the hearts of all who watched her there.
My aged ears still hear the faint refrains
that songs of Astrahahan so softly chime,
while through the slowly falling summer rains
a thousand orchids' scent still fills the air.

And as I sleep, I feel desire grow
from memories rewoven dream on dream
into a single brightly braided stream
to walk again beyond the fields we know.

Mythic Purity
From a story by Tanith Lee

The promised glow of spring's returning dawn
foretells of coming days when, from its light
the gold will grow to green on every lawn,
as spring's rebirth defeats the fading night.
A time when forest weaves its verdant wall
about a pool, wherein cerulean sky
is mirrored in a deeper blue than all
the seas or sapphires set before the eye
of hopeful wanderers, by such wonders drawn.

This mere lies ever deep within the hall
of woodland's woven master of light;
where seldom shall the wanderer's camp light fall
upon its silvered surface in the night.
For if such seekers of the wondrous fawn
could find this shining mirror of the sky,
and watch beside its banks at break of dawn,
their faith might meet a test to verify
that purity has power to cleanse us all.

Here, to this pool, as summer first draws nigh,
a fable comes to answer thirst's cool call;
to sip unsullied waters, and to sigh
amidst the green embrace of forest's shawl.
Here, far from trodden ways, where mankind's spite
is answered not with love but might of brawn,
a myth lives on, untouched by mortal fright
of those unanswered questions from the dawn
of time, that unawakened minds must still decry.

River of Stars

With boundless grace he glides, as if in flight,
on cloven hoof as light as first snowfall;
while sunrise hues pay homage to that white
of purity that cloaks him overall.
Beneath the brow, an amethystine eye
beholds the mere asleep midst grassy awn;
and starlight silver horn arcs down from high
to stir reflections of the vernal dawn,
as unstained lips refresh his virtue's might.

Dawn comes and wakes the land like Gabriel's horn
might wake mankind on Resurrection Day.
Shy movement shows the bed whereon he lay,
all white and pure as Mary's babe, newborn:
                    - this fabled Unicorn.

Navajo Weaver

Creativity on a desert-wood loom.
Three concurrent thoughts,
in the background the vision of the finished rug,
in the foreground the details of the current weft
and its dance with the vertical warp
and, like a champion chess player
seeing many moves ahead,
in the middle lies the process
      - Where will I blend the next thread?
      - How and where does the pattern change?
      - What colors, and when?

A juggler, three mental balls in the air;
no directions, no drawings or designs;
just the image of the finished piece
floating at the edge of thought,
flowing from the fingers,
thread by thread, with the racing shuttle:

Warp and weft,
shuttle and shed,
heddle and reed;
the coarse wool blends,
until Two Grey Hills glow.

The River of Stars

It is a cold night.
The moon is so new
that even its Cheshire grin is hidden.

I stand alone
on the last section of the dock,
beneath the black sky.

The constellations of the Zodiac,
Leo, Virgo, Libra, Sagittarius,
march above my head,
adorned in countless stars.

The great river of the Milky Way
teems with sparkled light.

The Weaver Girl & The Cowherd,
lovers of Ancient Japan,
are separated by this stellar river.

In tears they wait Orihime's Promise
- a bridge of magpies
on which to cross the star-filled flood.

One thousand three hundred sixty years
since Emperor Koken
made this story famous.

A blink of a gnat's eye
beside the stretch of time
that spans the boundless heavens.

Song of the Selkie
La Chanson de la Siréne

Once there was a boy
who lived beside the sea, high up on a cliff,
above the breakers, and the narrow beach.

Each day he'd walk the narrow beach,
searching for shells, driftwood,
treasure from a sunken pirate ship.

Each day he'd climb among the breakers,
collecting seaweed, limpets, and mussels,
for his evening chowder.

He lived alone on his cliff-top,
his mother dead in childbirth,
his father drowned at sea.

Sometimes they came to him,
what little vignettes he remembered
that still lived in his distant memory,

and then he sang of them, above the waves roar,
using the rhythm of their crash to punctuate his song,
using the soft wash of returning waves to feed the rhyme.

    Then one day his life changed.

as he walked the beach, singing,
he heard his song returned,
and he searched all day for that refrain.

That night he dreamed of a silver seal
gliding before an endless beach,
smooth and sleek, with seaweed streaming.

Each day, he heard the song,
each night he had the dream,
each morning they drew him back to the shore.

When the storms came,
and the great waves covered the narrow beach with spume,
he saw in them a maiden's hair flying;

and in the crash of the wave
on the rocks beneath his cliff
he heard the soft song crying.

When the storm left,
and the sun rose bright,
he found bare footprints on the sand.

Days came and went,
storms rose and fell, season flowed to season,
but the song continued, the dream remained.

    Then one day his life changed.

When he awoke, he heard the song.
Looking down, far down, to the rocks beneath the cliff,
seated upon a great boulder, he saw the singer;

her long hair flowing bright in the breeze,
wrapping around her naked body when the wind settled,
streaming out when it blew.

She sang the sea's song,
eerie and sweet, harsh and harrowing,
varying as the wind rose and fell.

The song of the Siren, it called to him,
it drew him to the beach,
it drew him to the boulders.

She turned, as she sang, and saw him,
she smiled, as she sang, and called him.
and as she sang, he came near.

She was beautiful, with auburn hair flying,
her clear skin the cream of mother of pearl,
her bright eyes the green of a storm-tossed sea.

As he came near, her song softened,
the green light grew in her eyes,
and she beckoned as she slid into the sea.

    And his life changed.

Youth's Passage

My time had come to wait within the grove,
to fast and dream, to wander in my mind
and find the spirit that would walk my ways,
would dye the threads that both our fates entwined.
And when you came our braided lives were woven
into the darkness of the night's embrace.
You soared on soundless wings beneath the sky
and drifted down the greenwood's lightless maze
in graceful silence, like a shadow's sigh
across the image of the forest's face.

Though once adrift, my future now is whole.
I now return into the fields of man.
Yet ever in the dark I live again,
a questing owl with freedom in my soul.

Night's Mysteries

Cloudless, the high night sky,
Ink-black, a million lights
shimmering and sparkling,
the white river of stars dividing.

The wind in the pines
- a bow on strings,
bare limbs, like castanets,
tap and clatter in counterpoint,
the driven waves mutter and murmur
as they nibble at the stony shore.

How many years has that song been sung,
the wind and the waves as they rise and fall
in the embrace of a dark November night?

What thought the Odawa,
in his smoke-filled, bare bark hut
when the fall storm rose to warn of winter?
The settler, in his flame-lit, log cabin,
where did his imagination roam in the night?

When the wild music of the forest plays,
where does man find his place?
Not in the howl of the wolves,
or the hoot of the owl.

For in the night, mystery is strong;
flame shadows flicker in the smoke,
spinning in wanton splendor
in the hidden corners of rough-hewn walls;

all the creatures of our dreams
peer out into the world of man,
and we shiver in wonder at
the figments of fear that dance
from the depths of our unknown.

Hunter and Hound

Thin clouds streaming,
hazy moon hanging
in the Sycamore.

The Hunter, hound at his heels,
spies through the branches,
at the Grecian beauty

of Selene and the Pleiades.
Underfoot, mud squelches
on a mid-March evening.

Seasons at Edo
(A Choka drawn from
"One hundred views of Edo"
by Hiroshigi)

Ukiyo-e
preserved the life of Nippon.
As art transcends time,
each picture marks a place,
history, and image,
the story of a people.

> The aged Doshin
> gave us his city's beauty
> graced by season's touch.
>
> Silken threads of rain,
> summer shower's silver touch,
> ribbons on a bridge.
>
> Streamers dance on autumn's wind,
> bamboo leaves mock birds
> when stars of fate are meeting.
>
> Winter's late weaving,
> bamboo robed in velvet white;
> three sparrows chatter.

Hiroshigi shares through time
the hidden faces of Edo.

Hidden Women of the Sea

The hidden women of the sea
that play within its cobalt well,
shall dance throughout eternity.

The few that meet them all agree
their beauty has no parallel,
the hidden women of the sea.

With form, in azure finery,
just glimpsed above the rising swell,
they dance throughout eternity.

When storm winds scream across the scree
and sea and rock toll, as a bell,
the hidden women of the sea

send their creamy tresses free
to fly above the wave's curved shell,
to dance throughout eternity.

And when they reach lands boundary,
whose sandy face they love so well,
the hidden women of the sea

sing out in voice of empathy
for those who cannot know the spell
to dance throughout eternity.

These words are shaped to be
a simple song – a villanelle,
where hidden women of the sea
can dance throughout eternity.

The Dancing Stars
(An Iroquois legend presented
as a sonnet in dactylic tetrameter)

The Iroquois Indians tell an old tale
about seven brothers who, sleeping one night,
were awakened by song, so graceful and frail,
yet with beauty embodied in musical sight.

The song was so lovely, its spirit so strong,
that they rose and were led to dance in its light;
and as it receded, it drew them along
into the splendor of heaven's great height.

One brother grew fearful as he looked below
and fell from eternity, into the night;
his spirit, however, still knew the song's flow,
now his body, a pine tree, still reaches for light.

And that is why six stars is all that you see
as the Pleiades shine through eternity.

Autumn Morning

Autumn morning dawns.
High in the western sky,
pink cloud-towers soar
to face the rising sun.
A gentle southern breeze
sends leaves sailing.
Dried sycamore leaves,
curled by nature's touch,
move by like ocean yachts
with foresails furled
and mainsails filled,
sailing across the western sea
from the fair world of faerie,
carrying their departed heroes
to the isles of Avalon.

Destiny

Past, present, and future,
Urd, Verdandi, Skuld,
Clotho, Lachesis, Atropos,
Spin, measure and cut.

Spinning the thread of life
the Weaver lays out her tapestry.
Spinner of silk, Grandmother Spider
weaves her web of fate.

Birth, life, and death,
Artemis, Selene, Hecate
Maiden, Mother, Crone;
the Triad is every-when.

Their shuttle weaving,
with Time's patterns
and the threads of souls,
the warp and weft of destiny.

Voices

Somewhere a shaman sings his
song and dances. Coyote,
out upon the prairie's lawn,
prances to the mournful notes
his children sing, while in the
dark, their music rings, and voices
of distant pasts cry out in
memories that do not last.

III
Memories

Walking with Granddad

Last Sunday was a dappled day, and high
above, white clouds strolled through the bright
blue landscape of the sky, while below
the scattered sunlight filtered through the new
green leaves of spring to clothe the stony stream
bed with a flowing gauzy garment, softly
woven out of lightness and of shadow.

It brought to mind another day, so many
years ago, when I was eight, and you
would take me walking on the banks of Ten
Mile Creek, and tell me of the days when you
were just as young as I was then,
a boy who only three years earlier
had made that long sea voyage from the distant
shores of what now seemed a different world.

You told of when you too had roamed these woods,
a wilder land, before the city had
grown near, when April skies ran deep and clear.
We talked of summer days upon the lake;
of fish we'd catch, and swimming in the sun,
and chilly autumn nights before the fire
with the sweet scent of apples roasting there.

And so, as many boys, my weeks were filled
with waiting for the joys of those bright days.
All the while your presence memories made,
that creep from out the corners of my mind
when the rain comes down to beat its ragged drum
upon the roof, or sunlight sifts between
the new green leaves to stride across the stream.

Questions of a Ten Acre Woods

Where are the woods I walked in as a child?
Where rabbits hid in leaves, wind-piled
between the fences and the trees;
where squirrels played upon the branches
without fears of men,
and hid their acorns as they'd done long ages
before the bustle of the city entered there,
before the halting hand of man could write
an end to all the cycles of those years.

Now here, houses stand instead of oaks.
A shopping mall has spread its walls where graceful
sycamores once grew. The days of the woods
and all its myriad lives are through.
Gone the fence-draped grapes,
the sweet, tart mixture of their taste
is but a distant memory.
Gone the bittersweet,
the bush that bore its orange berry
now lies beneath concrete.

Is this the world the children
of tomorrow yearn to know?
Where will they go to learn
to share the largess of the forest's
summer pantry? To watch
the green world grow?
Or must they seek fulfillment
by looking past the gantry
where Discovery now waits to ride
its tower of flame into the sky
and leaving, throw their wasted world
upon the midden of the universe?

Fjord Wings

The fjord is filled with wings today
of feather and fabric and foam.
Feathered wings are white and grey
and mark where the seagulls roam.
Fabric wings, in triangular pairs,
sail to and from their home.
While the wings of foam are the mermaid's hair
as it trails from the breaker's comb.

The Old Mill
Akrafjorden, Norway

The old mill stands abandoned here
among the fields of bracken.
Its weathered walls are without care,
the wooden wheel lies broken
with softened pieces scattered where
the voice of time has spoken,
as emerald moss, without roots that snare
is eating all that's oaken.

The river plays among the rocks
and down the race comes flowing.
Its snow-fed waters spill on blocks,
once old mill stones, now showing
the cracks of winters icy shocks.
They speak of times when growing
the grain once sold from nearby docks
still kept this old mill going.

But now the farms have gone away,
there's wilderness returning.
Their meagre yields just could not pay
enough to still the yearning
of the younger generation's day.
Time's wheel keeps on turning
as wind and rain grind out decay
and twilight skies are burning.

Blue Wax Day
Ørsdalen, Norway

The morning brought a crisp, clear winter day.
A blue wax day, below the freezing point.
A perfect day, with high above a clear
blue winter sky. Last night's winter dewfall left
two finger's worth of fresh, dry powder on
the little valley's open, frozen floor,
a shallow hollow in the high plateau
where summer's red-ripe berries once could win
their way to sunlight, now deep filled with snow,
where ptarmigan can hide among the drifts.

Two sundogs flank an icy circle's rim
that spins its ring around the sun's white face,
while my two hickory skis so lightly skim
through talc-soft snow and know the land's embrace.

Quiet Evening

The twilight dies, and dusk is gone.
I sit before the fire
and listen as reels go round,
Bjørling never seems to tire
of meeting Mimi, or singing of
the tragic love he's found
for Tosca or Manon.
Like him, I cannot tire of listening
to the sweet beauty that Puccini heard.
It rises softly from his music,
ringing with a soaring melody, offered
before the throne of Polyhymnia.

Outside the door, the winter wind is back
to raise its varied voice in mournful song.
This year it comes too soon to stack
the birch tree's leaves before my gate.
The fire has set another finger
slyly creeping around the oaken log
where plans of conflagration seem to linger
before the consummation of their mutual fate.

Here I sit and wish I too had known the song
to woo those gentle eyes and sable hair.
The music of your life was much too strong
for one like I to hope to settle there.
The love you had to give was for mankind.
Yet I refused to see; and sought to find
that thing that I might grasp
to set upon some pedestal,
as if it was of porcelain cast.

Too late I learned that I must freely give
the world your song as you would sing.
And now I only have one wish,
the happiness your songs of love can bring.

All My life, There Has Been Music

"… what is music, but a little wrinkling of air."
From Gwilan's Harp, by Ursula K. LeGuin.

All my life, there has been music.
When I was young, I played…
piano, clarinet, oboe, guitar.

Then, I didn't want to practice.
I'd rather shoot baskets
or ride my old, red Roadmaster.

Then I took a different turn
at one of life's crossroads
and put that all away…
        I thought.

But it never left.
Still it soars between my ears.

Somehow the song comes out;
notes become syllables,
cadence turns to meter…
    andante, allegro,
      lento, largo.

Harmony,
sometimes discordant,
sometimes not,
is heard as rhyme…
    stressed or unstressed,
      sight or slant,
        end-stopped or embedded.

Some say I write poetry.
Perhaps...
    but in reality
I make music using words.

Oman

I remember
- the heat of Muscat,
      108 degrees F at 8am,
- salty olives for bar food,
- silver, Maria Theresa thalers,
      for currency in the souk,
- Omani Bedouin
      wandering through the souk, their flowing dishdash
with brass-handled khunjar in the sash,
- beetled-brows of Portugese forts,
      Muttrah, Al Jalali and Al Milani, guarding the harbor
      entrances for four hundred years,
- helicopter ride over,
      crescent moons of massive dunes filling thousands of
      square miles of the Wahiba sands,
- hammerhead sharks
      schooling In Masirah bay,
- dining on one that evening
      on the offshore rig.

This is an ancient land
which history recognizes as Makkan,
traders of copper with Sumeria
four-and-a-half millennia ago.

Desert and sea coast,
nomad and fisherman,
two peoples came together.
Still evolving, they reach
across centuries, searching
for a new tomorrow.

Carcassonne

Thirty years ago,
I walked the narrow streets of Carcassonne,
beneath its high stone walls and towers,
over the grass-covered glacis,
up and down the moat's dry slopes.
A simple lunch in the courtyard cafe,
cheap red wine, cheese and croissant,
and in the evening listened
as the stones whispered legends.

Tales of Celts and Romans,
Moors and Cathars,
stone-age tales four millennia old,
romances of the Frankish years.

Through their telling, the night fell
as the ivory moon cast shadows
in the corners of the walls and arches
where spectral knights slept,
waiting for their fabled age to come again.

Campfire Reflections
Jenks, Oklahoma - September 2007

The wind whispers through the leaves and branches
of the oaks and maples that surround us;
the river grumbles as it slides along the bank,
stumbling over stones that lie scattered in its bed.
Beyond the fire's light, the crickets chatter,
and the peepers sing to the stars and moon above
that have given light to their night for endless ages.

Beneath the trees, in our hollowed pit, we hallow
the wonder of warmth and light that is the fire.
There, as they have through time, the Mongol's dragons
and the Norseman's trolls and giants peer out from the
crackling embers, and writhe in the rising flames.
All the wonders of the mythic past and the mysterious
future lie before us in a consuming light
that drives away the dark of our nightly fears.

In this cathedral of tall trees, mankind's life
has rested since Lucy walked out of her forest onto
the forbidding openness of some primeval plain.
It has been here, re-found from time to time
by men like Thoreau and Muir, Frost and Berry;
always present, still, aware, waiting
for those with courage to leave the loud world
and learn of solitude and of self, of belonging and of beauty.

Today, we crawl through crowded canyons of concrete
like columns of ants searching for the poisoned honey
of possessions and perceived power, never knowing
that we need no possessions, we already own the world.

What power could be greater than the power to hold it;
what responsibility could be greater than to protect it.

So come out, come to the embrace of the ancient forest
where, surrounded by sounds of wind and water and beast
you feel that solitude that lies in the silence of the soul
and learn that dominion holds obligation, not power.
Come to the quiet solitude of the endless plain,
where the infinite dome of the star-filled sky
endlessly enfolds your dreams and perceptions, where the
        green fire of aurora echoes the fires of your heart.

Old Flames

So many years I've traveled now
and through those years I've grown
accustomed to the simple fact
of dining out alone.

Yet often when I'm seated at
a table with my food
the muse will come and sit with me
to feed my pensive mood.

Not long ago I listened as
your song came back through time
and when I left, I found I had
a napkin filled with rhyme

that took me back a dozen years
to rend my heart in two.
A simple poem, offered here,
in memory of you.

> "Though love seems finally faded now,
> the memory's still there,
> of soft lips and warm embrace,
> clean fragrance of your hair;
>
> of city walks on sunlit days
> and lunches in the park,
> rainy nights by fire's light
> and loving in the dark.
>
> And though the heart's pain eases now,
> when I recall your eyes,
> the realization slowly grows;
> some flames are slow to die."

Goldfinch

I saw his colors flash by at nine,
an olive streak from pine to roof,
still dressed in winter drab.
By one he lay motionless on the deck,
breast fathers showing hints of summer gold,
black cap dulled in death.
No sign of what had stilled
the trill of vernal joy.

Anniversary
28 October 1999

For many years my life was solitary
filled with others literature and rhyme,
and in this world there never seemed the time
to find another soul with whom to marry
all my visions and my hopes, all the plans
that made the efforts of my life worthwhile,
to amplify my living with a smile
I could not find alone, by heart, or hands.

A thousand days ago that all was changed.
For then the fates relented, and arranged
to introduce a daughter and a wife,
and so reweave the pattern of my life,
      converting thus the rhythms of its poem
      into the living fabric of this home.

We Survived It

To those good old days
when the beer flowed easy,
when the games were played
but we never got queasy,
when the bands were loud
and the music was noisy,

    And whatever we did
    we survived it.

When the roads were long
and the cars were fast,
when we all were high
but we never crashed,
when the girls were hot
and we never came last,

    And whatever we did
    we survived it.

The days may be gone
but the memories stay,
are bellies have grown
and our hair is grey,
though the girls are older
the bands still play,

    For whatever we did
    we survived it.

Golden Pagoda

Its golden stupa, rising over the city
is seen for miles in every direction.
the sunlight sends its prismatic rays
coruscating from its diamond tip
like the lessons of Gautama Siddhartha.

Perched on its hill,
sheltering the eight hairs of Buddha,
fourteen hundred bells murmuring in the breeze
it has stood for twenty-six hundred years.
I walked its streets some years ago,
climbed the stairs between the lion guards,
strolled among the shops and shrines
that cluster around its crowded base,

    Shwedagon – the beating heart of old Rangoon.

Remembering Your Birthday
8 December 1945

Standing here on the shore,
looking out across the dark lake,
house lights reflected in its mirror,
watching faint stars shimmer
through high ice clouds,
the waning moon
rising over my shoulder
paints the frosted grass silver.

Remembering the warmth of late spring,
murmuring water
falling from pond to pond,
koi rising to feed,
hornets buzzing
as they chew the cellulose
from the weathered wood bench
to mold their paper home

and you nearby,
laughing at some private joke
as you weed the beds
and prune the azaleas
in the gardens that you loved.

IV
Morning Thoughts

Three AM

Three Am, awake again.
The seven syllable poems
of Shih Wu echo softly
from his mountain hut.
Here, the shore lights
sparkle on calm water.

Quiet Forest

The forest is quiet this morning,
tall pines disappear into blue fog,
beneath, the may-apples are beaded with dew.
As the rising sun clears the world's edge,
it turns the fog golden, the dew to diamonds,
and the forest fills with songs of life.

Southbound Geese

October sunset,
yellow sky shading orange.
Silhouetted geese,
grey against the fading sky,
their sharp angles pointing south.

Wind in the Pines

The water is calm tonight
Pine winds whisper Buddha's thoughts
Meditation mends the mind
Delusion's poison is cleared
by attachments last release
Thus, the real world is fulfilled.
The master sits in the Way
never seeking, always there.

Bright Days

Bright days have grown to long years.
Still, I watch the evening sun
setting red over the lake,
the stars filling the velvet sky.

The west wind sings in the pines.
The wren's song wakes me.
All these things are my teachers
of the infinite moment.

Daily Life

The lake spreads out before me.
Warm in the summer sunshine
Frigid in the winter wind
Wearing leaf-plaid in autumn
Fresh green garments in spring.
Daily life flows around me.
for my tomorrow is but
His today – eternally.

Thoughts on Non-attachment

I

One does not teach by wise action,
for action is fueled by attachment,
Attachments are the shackles
of the observed world.

The Teacher meditates on
non-attachment, becoming
free from its confining grasp.
Wisdom teaches by example.

II

The wind carries white clouds
and storm clouds but owns neither,
It embraces the tall pine's dance
then moves on to other tasks.

The crane flies unfettered skies.
The crow freely sings his joy.
Owning nothing, sharing all
is the heart of these lessons.

Cherry Season

Fifty years of driving southwards
from the Bay's cherry orchards.
Fifty years of spitting pits
from the cars rolled-down windows.

But for the roadside mowers
we would have an aisle of trees,
white blossoms every spring
stretching out a hundred miles.

Great Wave of Kanagawa

Great wave of Kanagawa,
reaching out with claws of foam.
Trough riding, between the swells
man is insignificant.

Fuji's perfect cone, afar,
mirrored by the nearby wave.
Blue and white, sea and mountain,
echo oceans immensity.

The Cusp of Now

Flowing springs feed the clear lake
blue beneath blue, cloud mirrored
Tree-covered hills, sand and stone,
earth's grist, ground by the icy
mill of ancient ages past.
Time is flowing through us all,
always changing, never still.
Life lives on the cusp of now.

December Stories

Winter night, waning moon light
paints the wave tops silver.
North wind whistles through the tree's
barren arms, stripped of summer.

Torn clouds racing through the sky
reveal the scattering stars
that tell the timeless stories
of the legends of the world.

Norwegian Cliffs

Grey cliffs rise above the sea.
Grey-green tendrils, reindeer moss
wet with rain, beneath the trees.
Climbing the narrow ledges,
blue mist at my back, edges
falling away to distant
water, reflecting grey clouds;
Such clear memories of Norway.

Dance of Time

The dance of time spins down the flashing years
in happiness and sorrow, fear and joy,
while lives that measure days bob like a buoy
upon the endless ocean of our fears.

For expectations and attachments come
to bind us to this plane with chords of time,
until we make the oft-perceived crime
of shunning past and present for this day.

These words are written from an endless dream,
ideas flowing from the timeless void
to whence a life's experiences stream
to tumble out in ways defined by Freud.

You can't put words in the silent mouth of the muse,
and yet they ring through the memories we lose.

Perception's Flower

Sometimes I do not understand
the world I see;
the stationary earth
and the sun that encircles is illusion;
but so too, a stationary sun
with an encircling world.

Einstein spoke of relativity,
Buddha of perception.
The 'Gita called it all *maya*.
Ephemeral or illusory,
it is only the product
of individual experience.

Yet the experience is but the seed,
It is the flower
that grows from our perception
that defines us.

The Horns of Selene

The horns of Selene,
ivory hung in ebony,
November's waning crescent
floats above the leaf-strewn ground.

Gold and crimson leaves, now brown,
rain-matted from the fall storm,
feed the white crowns of mushrooms,
as form decays to feed new form.

The earth spins around the sun,
The seasons ride their cycle,
Wheels within wheels ever turning,
Each moment, life's single breath.

This Moment of You

"Not you in the moment.
But this moment of you…." (*)

It is not about life in the moment,
it is not about living in the moment, in time.
It us about life *as* the moment.

There is no past or future,
only this individual moment of existence
as the vehicle for Harmony's expression
on this physical plane.

Mindfulness is the recognition of,
the awareness of,
the experience of that expression.

(*) Godfrey Johns; *Ideas on Wing: #43; This Moment of Your Living;* Christian Science Publishing Society, Boston, Mass. 1978

Mindful

Even when closed,
My eyelids blink,
Twitching pink velvet
Lubricating the organ beneath.

Thus the universe works,
Maintaining itself;
Not formless chaos,
But timeless purpose.

Truth and Beauty

Truth is Beauty.
Beauty is Truth.

All reality is illusion.
Thus said Krishna to Arjuna.
But the illusion holds great Beauty;
Thus it also holds Truth.

Being exists not in the moment.
Being exists as the moment.
As the moment, the illusion
does not matter, only the Beauty.

This is the Beauty of being.
This is the Truth of existence.
As the moment, Life is endless
for, there, Time is the illusion.

Season's Ending

Another dark November night.
The north wind's voice is loud again.
Lights on the far shore are shrouded
by the cold mists and slanted rain.

This is the season of changes.
Autumn has not quite ended.
Brown leaves are daily falling
yet Winter's fist is knocking.

About the Author

Born and raised in Toledo Ohio, Leutz graduated from The University of Toledo in 1965 with a degree in Chemical Engineering. Following graduation, his professional career exposed him to a great deal of travel, ultimately providing the opportunity to visit all fifty states and nearly forty countries on five continents. During this career, he moved often, including ten years living in Norway. Upon returning to the United States in 1987, he settled in Tulsa, Oklahoma. After retirement in 2004, he spent time volunteering and serving as an officer with the Tulsa Chapter of the Sons of the American Revolution, as a docent at the Nature Conservancy's Visitor Center of the Tall Grass Prairie Preserve, and also at the Thomas Gilcrease Museum of American History and Art. In 2013, after the passing of his wife, he rebuilt and returned to his family's old summer home on a small lake in southern, Michigan. This is his third book. His interests, other than writing, are history, genealogy, and photography.

www.ingramcontent.com/pod-product-compliance
Lightning Source LLC
Chambersburg PA
CBHW022044160426
43209CB00002B/56